T0006680

Bruno
the Beekeeper

A Honey Primer

Aneta Františka Holasová

translated by Andrew Lass

CANDLEWICK PRESS

For my grandfather

Text and illustrations copyright © 2013 by Aneta Františka Holasová
Translation copyright © 2021 by Andrew Lass

All rights reserved. No part of this book may be reproduced, transmitted, or stored in an information
retrieval system in any form or by any means, graphic, electronic, or mechanical, including
photocopying, taping, and recording, without prior written permission from the publisher.

First US edition 2021

Originally published under the title *Lumír včelaři* by Labyrint (Czech Republic) 2013

Library of Congress Catalog Card Number pending
ISBN 978-1-5362-1461-1

CCP 26 25 24 23 22 21
10 9 8 7 6 5 4 3 2 1

Printed in Shenzhen, Guangdong, China

This book was typeset in Agenda.
The illustrations were done in watercolor.

Candlewick Press
99 Dover Street
Somerville, Massachusetts 02144

www.candlewick.com

Preface

In his heart and soul, Bruno is a beekeeper. But how did it all begin? When he was still a small bear, he enjoyed a carefree life full of mischief and fun, as is usually the case with little bears. He used a slingshot, he wandered outdoors, and he played in the forest, where he much preferred to be rather than in school.

One day he inherited bees from his old grandfather and started taking care of them. In the beginning it was not at all easy; it took a while before he and the bees made friends. Today Bruno is an experienced beekeeper. Grandma, whom you will meet, helps Bruno with beekeeping. She is kind, patient, and as hardworking as a bee.

Bees and Other Similar Flying Insects

hornet moth

hornet

wasp

hoverfly

fly

horsefly

bumblebee

queen bee

worker bee

drone

Worker Bees

The queen bee lays a fertilized egg in a cell (a chamber in a hive). After twenty-one days, a worker bee emerges from the cell and starts her life's work. She cleans cells; keeps the developing bees, called larvae, warm and feeds them; cleans the hive; draws and processes nectar from flowers into honey; tamps pollen into cells; and builds combs. Then she leaves the hive to act as a guard. There must be enough worker bees to guarantee a sufficient amount of honey and pollen for all the bees to eat. Worker bees try out all these jobs during their short lifetime, and after about forty days, they die.

The Metamorphosis of a Worker Bee

A translucent white egg, about one-sixteenth of an inch (1.5 millimeters) long, is attached by its narrowest end to the bottom of a cell.

The egg begins to lean sideways.

The egg lies at the bottom of the cell as a larva develops inside it.

The larva fills the bottom of the cell and curls up so that its two ends just about meet.

The larva grows a bit. Worker bees feed it a substance called royal jelly, as well as a mixture of honey, pollen, and water.

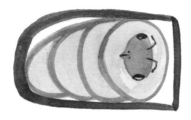

A worker bee caps the cell. The larva changes its position so its head is pointing toward the exit.

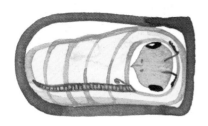

The larva changes into a prepupa. A quiet time begins.

The perfect pupa

The metamorphosis of the larva into an adult is complete after twenty-one days.

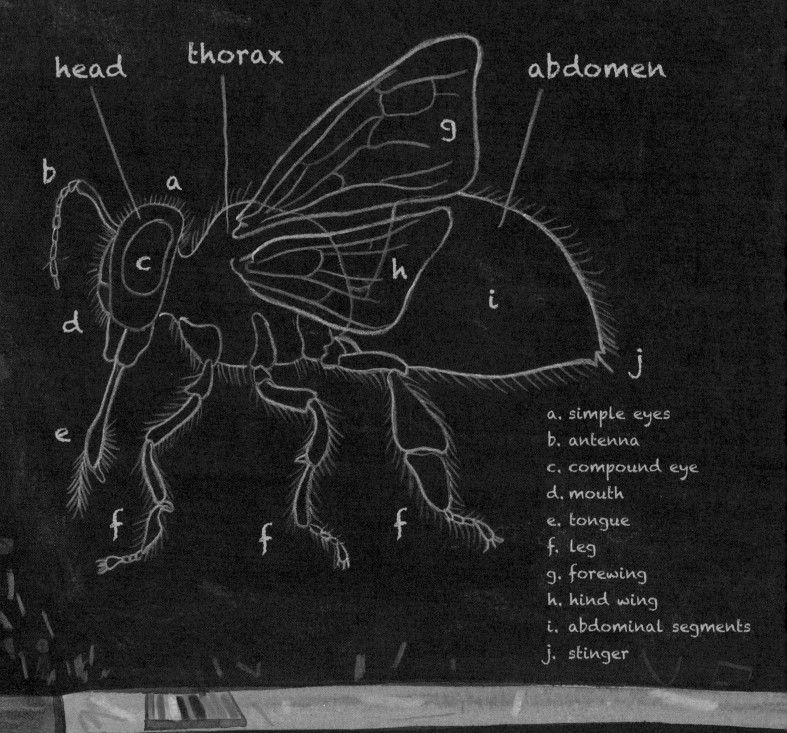

worker bee

head

thorax

abdomen

a. simple eyes
b. antenna
c. compound eye
d. mouth
e. tongue
f. leg
g. forewing
h. hind wing
i. abdominal segments
j. stinger

The Anatomy of a Bee

head

a. eyes

b. antennae

c. mouth

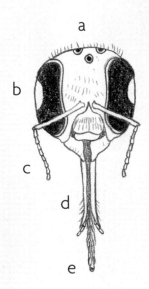

a. Simple eyes. Three small eyes form a triangle at the top of the bee's head and provide orientation in relation to the sun.

b. Two large eyes composed of thousands of tiny eyes take in the world around the bee.

c. A bee's antennae detect scents and air currents.

d. A bee's mouth has two jaws called mandibles, which she uses to manipulate and chew wax, pollen, and propolis (a gluey resin that bees use when building a hive).

e. Tongue. Enables the bee to suck in nectar. It is about ¼ inch (5–7 millimeters) long.

foreleg

a. antenna cleaner

middle leg

a. spur

b. pollen brush

c. suction pads

hind leg

a. pollen brush

b. pollen press

c. pollen basket

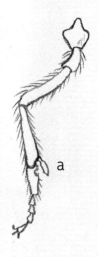

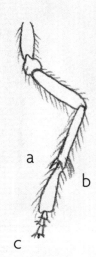

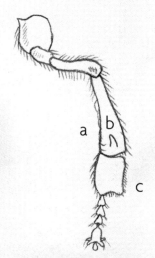

7

The Life of a Worker Bee

On days one and two, she cleans cells and keeps the larvae warm.

Days three through ten, she feeds larvae.

Days six through twelve, she cleans the hive and other bees.

Days ten through fifteen, she receives and processes nectar.

Also days ten through fifteen, she packs pollen into cells.

Days twelve through eighteen, she builds combs.

Beginning with day fifteen, she leaves the hive and explores her surroundings.

On days seventeen and eighteen, she acts as a guard.

Days twenty through forty, she collects pollen and nectar.

8

After about forty days,
she dies.

Drones

Male bees are called drones and develop from unfertilized eggs. The adult male leaves its cell and goes with other drones to a gathering place to attract a queen. The main job of a drone is to preserve the bee stock by passing on sperm to a queen bee. After mating with a queen, the drone dies.

The Metamorphosis of a Drone

The egg sits at the bottom of the cell.

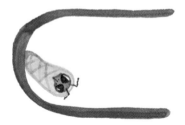

The egg begins leaning to the side.

The egg lies at the bottom of the cell.

As the larva hatches from the egg, worker bees feed it royal jelly.

As the larva fills out the bottom of the cell, it curls up so that its two ends meet.

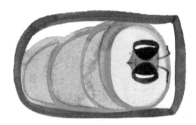

Then the larva straightens out. The cell is capped.

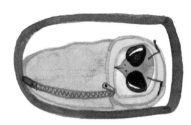

A period of rest begins. The larva morphs into a pupa.

The pupa is fully formed.

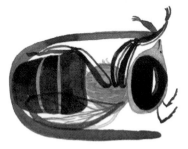

After twenty-four days, the adult crawls out of the cell and immediately demands to be fed by the worker bee.

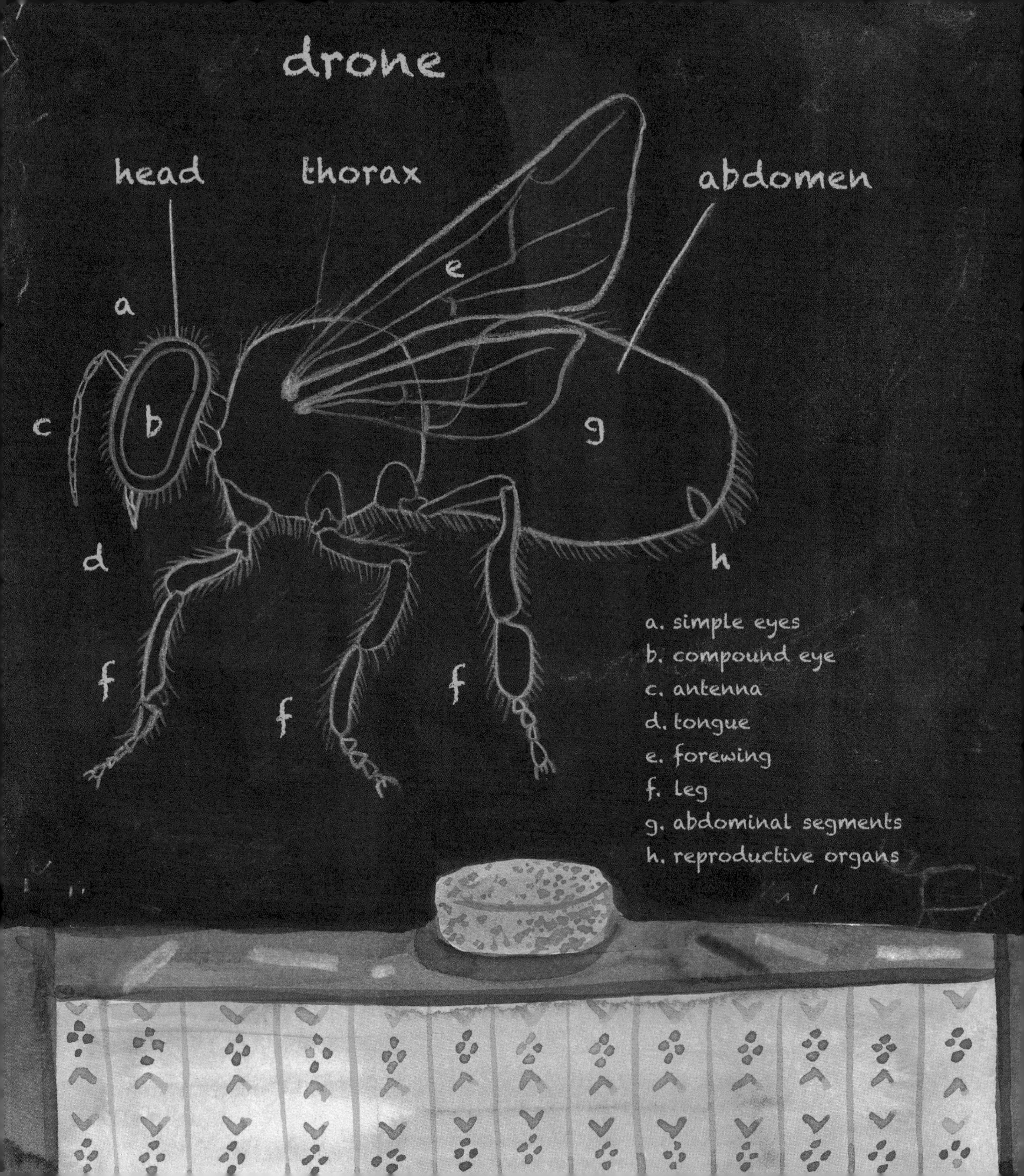

drone

head   thorax   abdomen

a

e

c

b

d

g

f   f   f

h

a. simple eyes
b. compound eye
c. antenna
d. tongue
e. forewing
f. leg
g. abdominal segments
h. reproductive organs

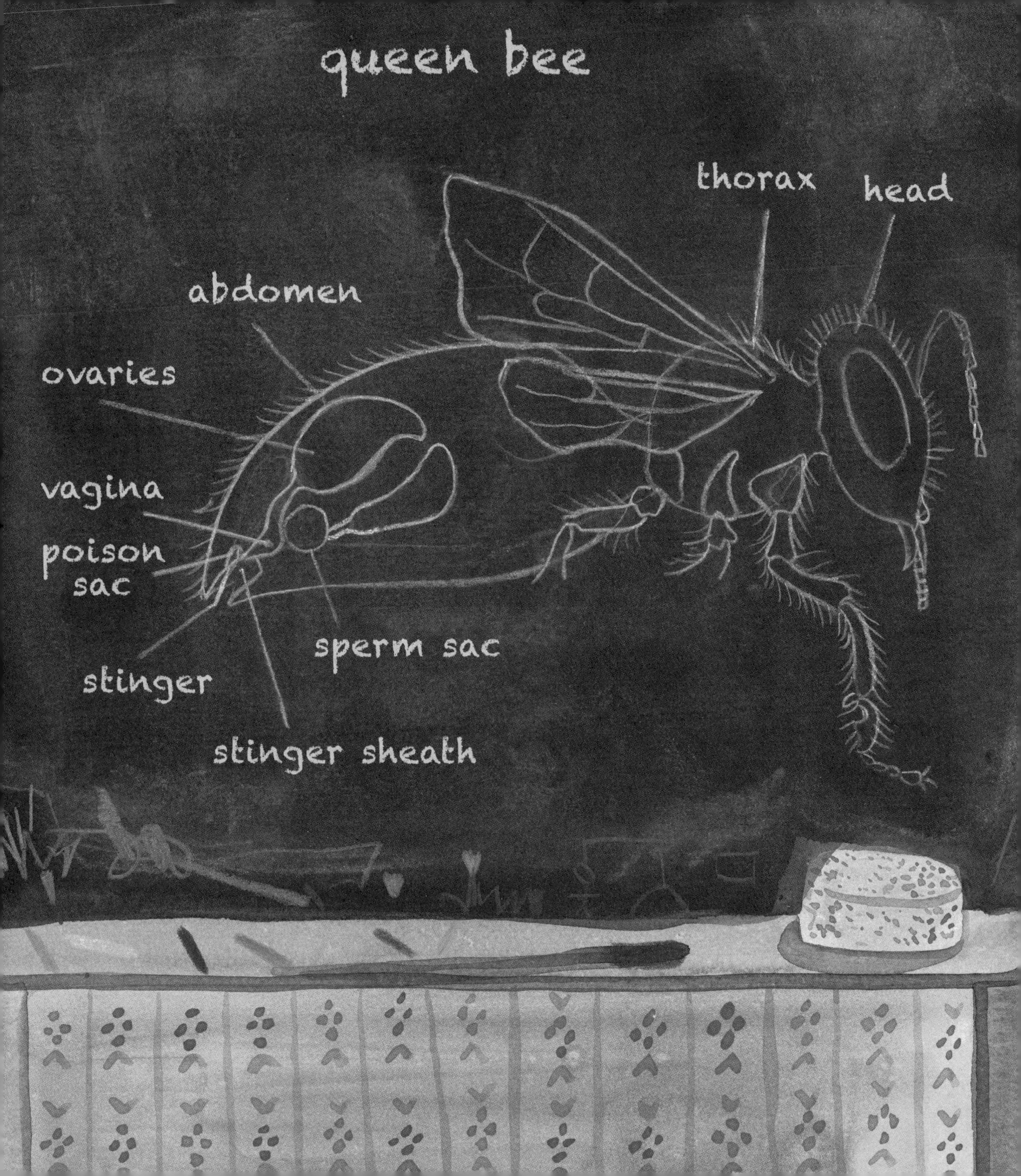

queen bee

thorax

head

abdomen

ovaries

vagina

poison
sac

sperm sac

stinger

stinger sheath

The Queen Bee

A queen bee develops from a fertilized egg in a special queen cell built from wax by the worker bees. The future queen is fed exclusively with royal jelly until she becomes a pupa. Fifteen days from the time the egg was laid, the new queen leaves the queen cell and replaces the hive's prior queen. The first excursion of the young queen is called her maiden flight. She flies to the drones' gathering place, where she mates.

She stores the sperm she receives from the drones in her sperm sac. After mating, she returns to the hive. She retains the sperm in her body throughout her life in order to fertilize the eggs she lays. Her main job is to lay eggs to provide her colony with a sufficient number of workers and drones to ensure the continuation of the bee colony.

The Metamorphosis of a Queen

The egg sits at the bottom of the cell.

The egg latches on to the edge of the cell and slowly leans to the side.

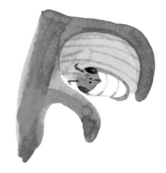

The egg becomes a larva; worker bees feed it royal jelly and build out the queen cell.

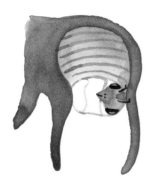

The larva grows and fattens until it fills the bottom of the cell.

Worker bees complete the construction of the queen cell.

Worker bees cap the cell with wax.

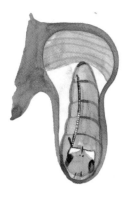

The larva wraps itself in a silken thread. During a period of quiet, the larva changes into a pupa.

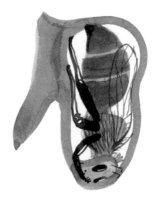

The pupa is almost fully formed.

The adult queen bee emerges after fifteen days.

15

The Hive and Its Parts

Bees in nature make their own hives in hollow trees. If you want to keep bees, you need to build them a hive with frames that will provide the spaces they need to hatch and make honey.

a. brood chamber
The main part of the hive

b. honey super
Added on top of the brood chamber
at the time of honey production

c. opening slot
The entrance to the hive

d. landing board
A small landing strip right under the slot

Frames

Frames are stacked inside the honey super. Frames are built from four thin slats. Grandpa preferred wood from the linden tree for his frames, but the slats can also be made of metal, plastic, or pine. The top slat is a bit longer at both ends, providing a handle for moving and hanging.

Spacers

Most frames have four spacers. They keep the frames equally apart so the bees can move freely between them.

Brood Chamber

The brood chamber is where eggs, larvae, and pupae develop. You can see the eggs and larvae in the open cells of the comb. The pupae develop in the closed—capped—cells.

Cells

Cells are little rooms within the wax honeycomb. Bees store pollen, nectar, honeydew, and honey in the cells, and they are also where bees develop.

Beekeeper's Clothing

If you want to start beekeeping, you will need protective clothing. See how spiffy Bruno looks in his beekeeping suit, hat, and veil. Bruno, however, is a bear beekeeper and has a thick fur coat, so he can work without a special protective suit.

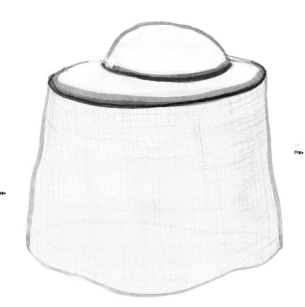

beekeeping hat

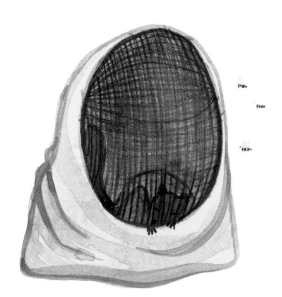

bee veil

gloves

Bee Parasites and Predators

hornet

wasp

ant

toad

field mouse

wax moth

tracheal mite

varroa mite

swallow

Late Summer and Fall

Removing the Supers

In late summer, Bruno the beekeeper removes the supers from the hives and prepares them for the next year. He must work very carefully and clean all the supers of the bits and pieces of old wax and propolis. When he's finished, he places them in the honey house. It is dry in there, and mice can't get to them.

Protecting the Drawn Combs

The empty combs that Bruno removed from the supers are stored in closets over the winter. To prevent wax moths from hatching in the combs, he freezes them before hanging them in the closet. They will be ready for further use after airing out.

wax foundation

pressed beeswax prepared for building the comb

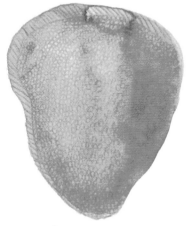

drawn comb

the comb bees build out of wax

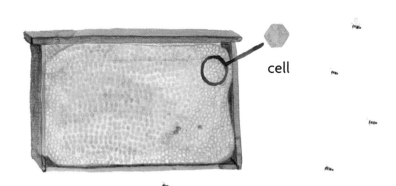

cell

honeycomb

a comb full of honey

dry comb

The honey has been extracted and the honeycomb has been air-dried.

Beeswax

Inside their bodies, worker bees transform honey and pollen into wax. The worker bees excrete wax from glands on the bottom of their abdomen. It takes the form of a tiny scale or flake. The bees then chew the wax with their mandibles. The chewing adds saliva and heat to the wax, making it soft. Then they can begin creating a new comb from the softened wax.

Bruno places old combs into a solar beeswax melter, where the wax softens and runs into a mold. He removes the mold and lets the wax cool off and congeal. He then sends the acquired wax out to a mill to be cleaned and made into comb foundations that Bruno will place on his frames.

Candles

Grandma makes candles from some of the comb foundations. She heats the foundation with a hair dryer so it can be shaped. She places a wick at the end, then wraps the foundation around it.

 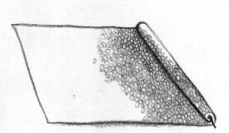 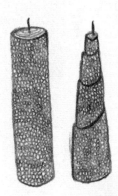

Propolis, Also Known as Bees' Cement

Some plants produce a gooey substance called resin, which bees collect and blend with saliva from their glands to make propolis. Propolis can be different colors, from a yellow green to a dark brown. Bees use it to cement openings and cracks in the hive and in the hive's entrance area and to strengthen a hive's cells. It kills bacilli, a kind of bacteria, helping to maintain hygiene in the hive. Also, if a mouse or a shrew gets into the hive, bees will kill the intruder. But they lack the strength to remove the animal, so instead they wrap the body in propolis so it doesn't decompose in the hive. Propolis offers defense against all sorts of contaminations.

Bruno scrapes propolis from the frames and supers and stores it. Grandma then makes a propolis tincture that she uses as a healing ointment for skin.

Propolis Tincture

Grandma mixes 3½ ounces of propolis with a quart of 60 percent alcohol. She lets the propolis dissolve in the alcohol for ten days and shakes the mixture every day. After ten days, Grandma pours it through a paper filter into a clean bottle.

Bee Feeding

When beekeepers remove honey from the hive, they must replace it with another food source. During August, Bruno supplements the bees' food supplies with a mixture of sugar and water. This is to be sure that they'll have plenty of food reserves so they will be nourished and strong to survive the winter.

Preparing the Sugar Solution

Grandma prepares the mixture of sugar and water. She carefully mixes two parts water with three parts sugar. She pours the mixture into jars and covers the jars with special lids with openings through which the bees can suck the liquid easily. The jars fit upside down in a round opening on the top of the hives.

Winter

Listening to the Bees

Winter is a time of rest for bees. The more peace and quiet Bruno gives them, the better. Several times during the winter, Bruno goes to check his hives by listening. All is well if the bees are humming.

Honey

Winter Work

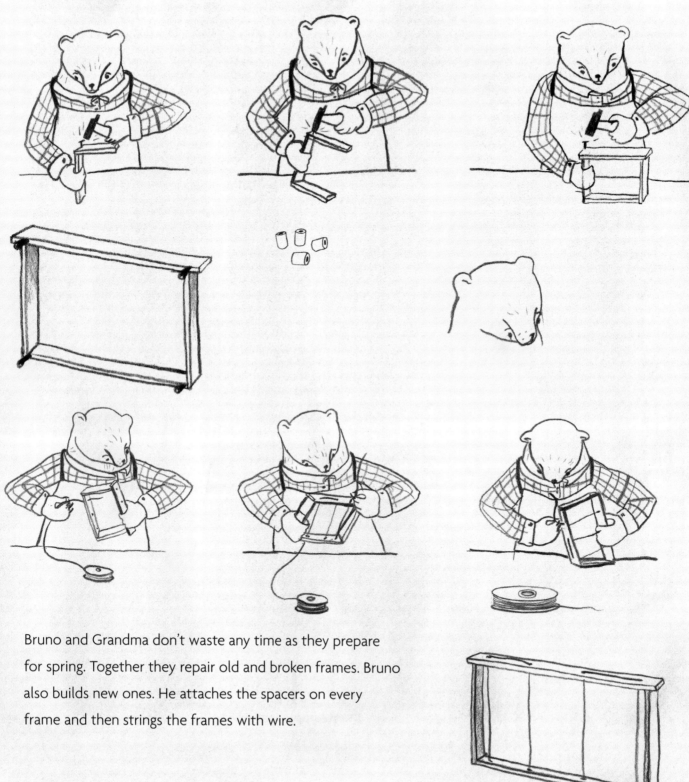

Bruno and Grandma don't waste any time as they prepare for spring. Together they repair old and broken frames. Bruno also builds new ones. He attaches the spacers on every frame and then strings the frames with wire.

Grandma helps him attach comb foundations on the strung frames by using electricity to slowly melt them onto the wires. While doing this she must be especially careful not to melt the wire all the way through the foundations. Grandma also washes the jars filled with sugar solution and cleans any traces of propolis that the bees may have left on the lids.

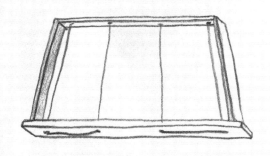

Spring

What flowers bloom in spring?

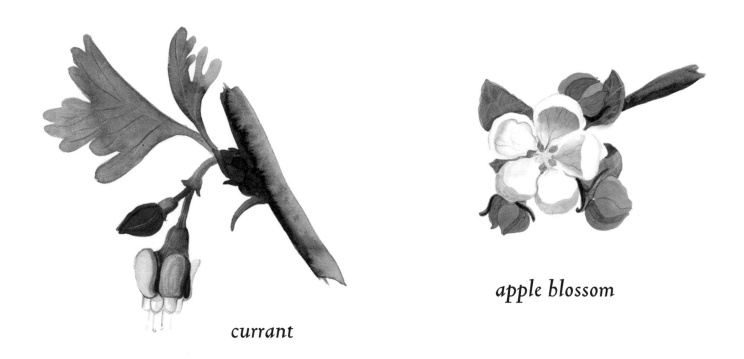

currant

apple blossom

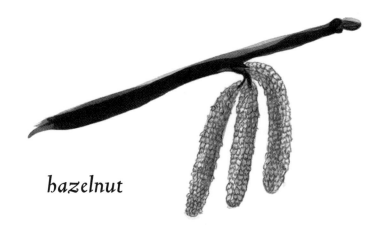

hazelnut

44

snowdrop

crocus

snowflake

liverwort

anemone

Supplemental Feeding of Bees in the Spring

In early spring, Bruno supplements the bees' food supplies since they likely do not have enough to eat when winter comes to an end. He makes a dough from sugar and honey extracted from his hives and places the sweet loaves on top of the frames in the hives.

Marking the Queen

Bruno is diligent about marking his queens.

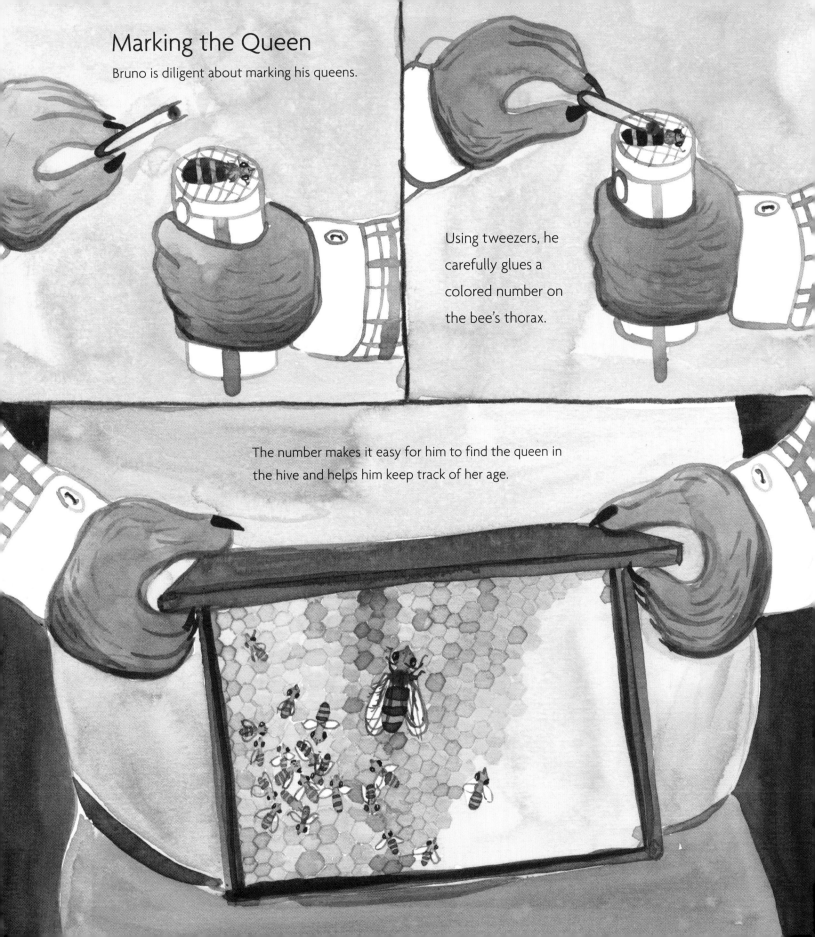

Using tweezers, he carefully glues a colored number on the bee's thorax.

The number makes it easy for him to find the queen in the hive and helps him keep track of her age.

Checking on the Bee Colony

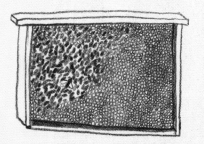

frame with a honeycomb

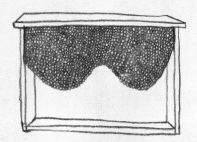

frame with a drawn comb

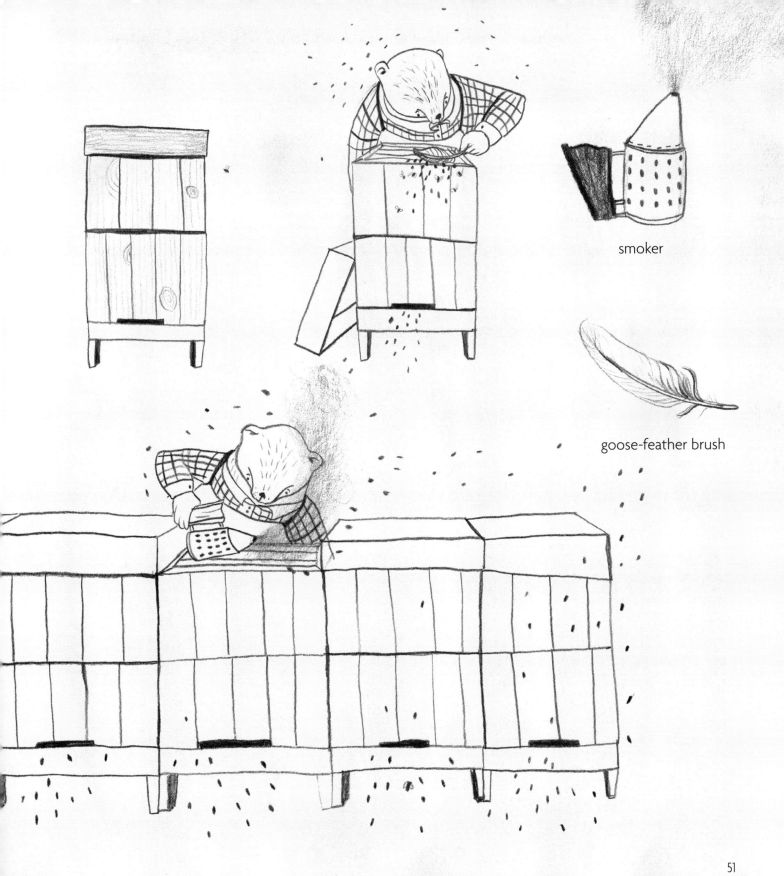

smoker

goose-feather brush

51

Supering Up

When the hives are filled with brood and the colony is strong enough, Bruno adds the supers to the hives. He places a queen excluder between the brood chamber and the super. This prevents the queen from getting into the super and laying eggs there. The super then contains only ripe honey for Bruno to extract.

Swarming

Swarming is a natural bee behavior. When a swarming mood starts brewing, the bees build and cap a new queen's cell. A swarm with the old queen then flies out from the hive. Sometimes a secondary swarm departs with a young, not yet fertilized queen bee. Swarms usually settle close to the hive, then Bruno collects them in a swarm trap. Swarming can be caused by the overpopulation of bees in a hive. To avoid this, Bruno monitors the brood-rearing and amount of honey stored in the frames. If the bee population in a hive is expanding quickly, he divides the brood into separate hives. If the bees don't have enough provisions, a hungry swarm can develop and the bees may move elsewhere. This can be avoided by replenishing the provisions.

Summer

What flowers bloom in summer?

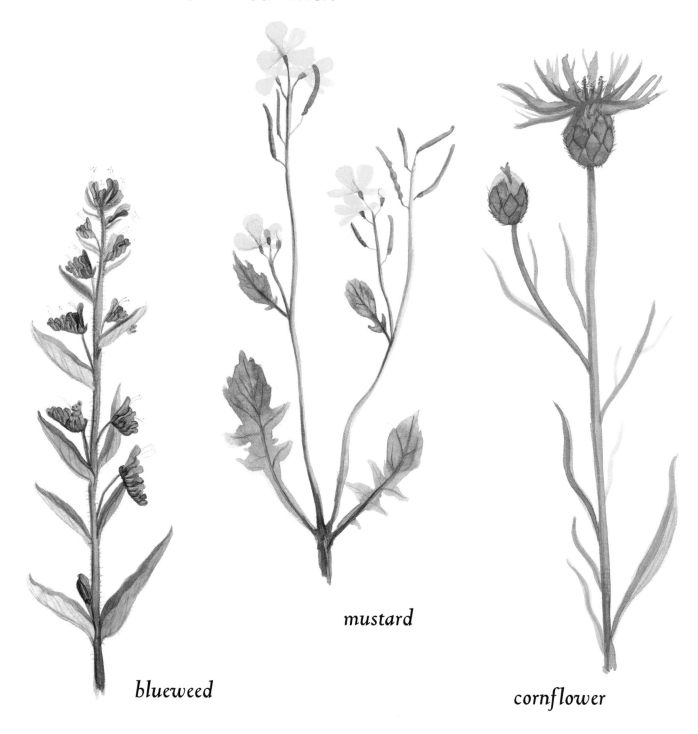

blueweed

mustard

cornflower

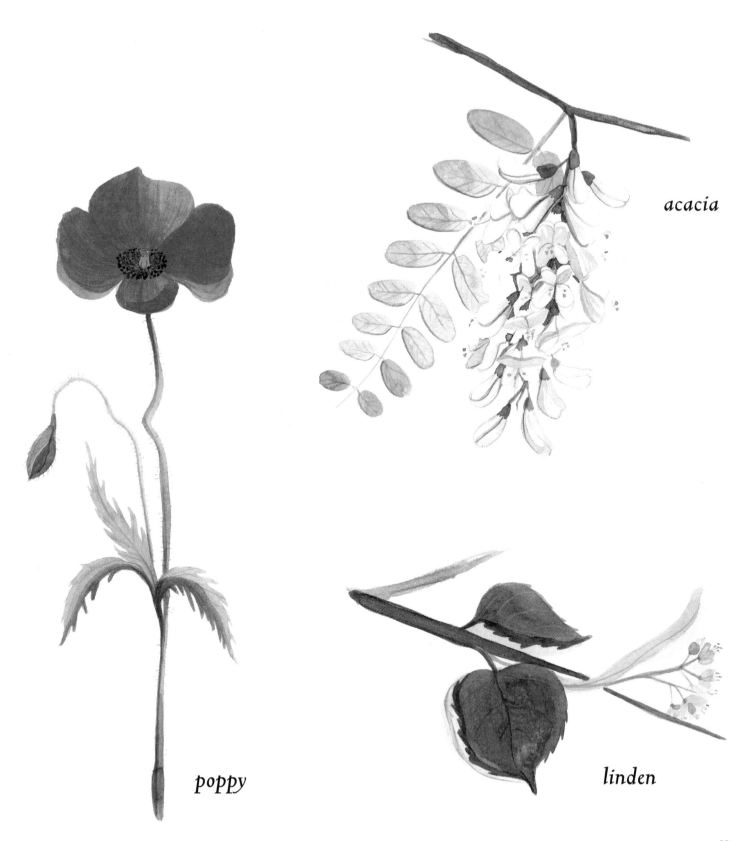

acacia

poppy

linden

Honey Harvest

Plants pollinated by bees and insects produce nectar. Bees collect this sweet nectar as a source of food and thicken it through evaporation. The thickened nectar becomes honey. Honey's color and scent is affected by the plants from which the bees collect nectar.

Bruno and his grandma harvest the honey in the extraction room. They uncap the honeycomb from both sides using a special fork (the cap is a thin layer of wax the bees use to enclose the honey in the cell). They must take care to avoid damaging the comb. As they work, they rest the frame with the comb on a stand so that any honey that drips out can run into a small tub underneath it and not a drop of honey is lost.

They place the frames with the uncapped combs into a honey extractor. Frames with honey-filled combs turn in the extractor as on a carousel. Honey flies from the individual cells, sticks to the walls of the extractor, and pours through a strainer out of an opening into a bucket. After extracting one side, they turn the frame around and extract again. While extracting, it is important to monitor the spinning speed in the honey extractor. The strainer removes pieces of wax and other debris so that the honey is pure.

Beeswax Chewing Gum

Bruno likes to give Grandma and the baby bears a piece of honeycomb to chew. It is a sweet and scented treat—yum! After they chew the honey out of the comb, they spit it out into the rest of the wax, which is further processed.

Honeydew

Honeydew is a substance with high sugar content excreted by sucking insects onto the surface of leaves and pine needles. Bees collect this liquid and transform it into honeydew honey. Honeydew honey can cause bees to get sick, so it is typically removed from hives before winter.

aphid   *honeydew*   *bee*

Honey Harvesting Tools

a. uncapping fork

b. spatula used to scrape honey from the comb

c. honey bucket

d. can for storing honey

e. strainer

f. frame stand

g. honey extractor

Bruno carries the honey-filled combs to Grandma
in the extraction room.

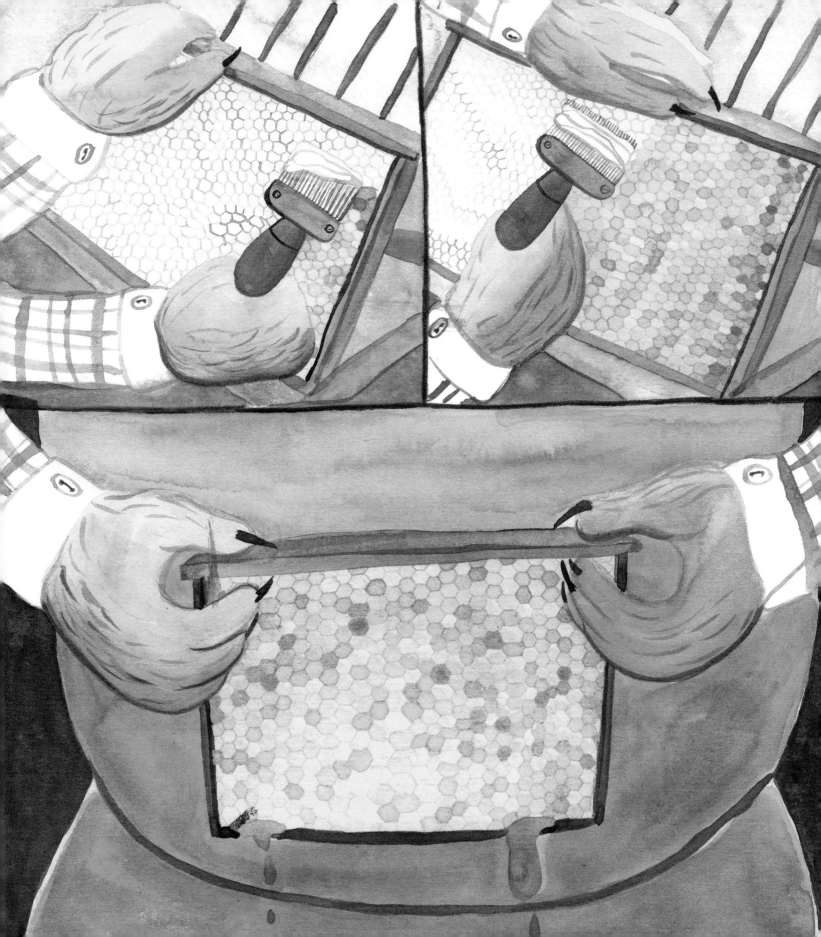

Gingerbread Cookies

If you'd like to make Grandma's gingerbread cookies, ask an adult to help. Makes 2 dozen cookies.

1½ cups honey
3½ cups fine whole-grain rye flour
1 cup confectioners' sugar
2 egg yolks
1 teaspoon baking soda
½ teaspoon baking powder
pinch of lemon rind
pinch of orange rind
pinch of sea salt
gingerbread spice mix

Gingerbread Spice Mix

Grandma grinds her own gingerbread spices so they are aromatic and fresh.

10 allspice corns
3 star anise pods
½ teaspoon cinnamon
5 cloves
pinch of ground ginger
½ teaspoon fennel seeds
½ teaspoon anise seeds

Grandma heats the honey in a double boiler, and when it is warm, she mixes in the flour. She allows the dough to cool down to room temperature before she mixes in all the other ingredients and places it in the refrigerator to chill for 3 hours. She preheats the oven to 325°F (160°C) and rolls out the chilled dough to about ¼ inch (6 millimeters) thick. Grandma sprinkles the rolling pin with flour to keep the dough from sticking to it. She places the cut-out gingerbread cookies on a baking sheet. Grandma uses parchment paper so they don't stick to the pan. Before she places the cookies in the oven, she brushes them with an egg-yolk wash. She bakes them for about 10 minutes, until they're golden brown. Enjoy!

Index